MW00483198

COCO CHANEL

Frances Lincoln Limited
74–77 White Lion Street
London N1 9PF
www.franceslincoln.com

A catalogue record for this book is available
from the British Library.

ISBN 978-0-7112-3717-9

1 2 3 4 5 6 7 8 9

FRANCES LINCOLN LIMITED
PUBLISHERS

COCO CHANEL

by Zena Alkayat and Nina Cosford

'I am not a heroine. But I have chosen the person I wanted to be.'

Coco Chanel, 1946

GABRIELLE CHANEL WAS BORN ON
19th AUGUST 1883 IN A CHARITY
HOSPITAL FOR THE POOR IN SAUMUR,
WEST FRANCE. HER FATHER ALBERT
WAS A ROVING MARKET TRADER,
HER MOTHER JEANNE WAS FROM
A WORKING-CLASS FAMILY.

Saumur

ABANDONED BY THE FAST-LIVING ALBERT WHILE PREGNANT WITH GABRIELLE'S OLDER SISTER, JEANNE SPENT HER LIFE CHASING AFTER HIM AS HE HOPPED BETWEEN MARKET TOWNS ACROSS FRANCE.

SOCIALLY EMBARRASSED, JEANNE'S
FAMILY COMPELLED ALBERT
TO MARRY HER IN 1884. HE
RELUCTANTLY AGREED, BUT THE
BOND OF MARRIAGE DID LITTLE
TO KEEP HIM BY HER SIDE.

The Chanel

Albert
b. 1856

Julia-Berthe
b. 1880

Gabrielle
b. 1883

Alphonse
b. 1885

Family Tree

jeanne
b. 1863

Antoinette
b. 1887

Lucien
b. 1889

Augustin
b. 1891

GABRIELLE AND HER SIBLINGS WERE
ACCUSTOMED TO HARD WORK, BAD
LIVING CONDITIONS AND A BROKEN
FAMILY LIFE, BUT THINGS BECAME
WORSE WHEN THEIR MOTHER DIED OF
BRONCHITIS AT 31. GABRIELLE WAS 11.

DESERTED BY THEIR FLY-BY-NIGHT
FATHER AND UNWELCOMED BY THEIR
MOTHER'S FAMILY, THE CHILDREN
WERE LEFT ORPHANED.

GABRIELLE'S YOUNG BROTHERS WERE
GIVEN TO A PEASANT FAMILY TO
PROVIDE FARM LABOUR IN RETURN
FOR BASIC KEEP.

GABRIELLE AND HER TWO SISTERS
WERE SENT TO A CONVENT ORPHANAGE
IN THE RURAL VILLAGE OF AUBAZINE.
SHE NEVER SAW HER FATHER AGAIN.

Aubazine

GABRIELLE FOLLOWED STRICT
RELIGIOUS DUTY, TOOK BASIC
STUDIES AND LEARNT NEEDLEWORK.

LATER AS AN ADULT SHE WOULD
BEND THE TRUTH AND DESCRIBE
A MISERABLE TIME SPENT IN
THE CARE OF 'WICKED AUNTS'
IN WHICH 'LOVE WAS A LUXURY
AND CHILDHOOD A SIN'.

GABRIELLE WOULD LOSE HERSELF
IN ROMANTIC STORIES TORN FROM
THE PAGES OF NEWSPAPERS.

ON TURNING 18, GABRIELLE WAS FINALLY FREE TO LEAVE AUBAZINE, TRANSFERRING TO ANOTHER CONVENT IN THE GARRISON TOWN OF MOULINS IN CENTRAL FRANCE.

HER AUNT ADRIENNE CHANEL WAS A FELLOW CHARITY PUPIL THERE. WITH JUST TWO YEARS BETWEEN THEM, SHE AND GABRIELLE BECAME AS TIGHT AS SISTERS.

AFTER A YEAR AT THE CONVENT,
GABRIELLE AND ADRIENNE TOOK JOBS
AND LODGINGS IN A DRAPERY.

THEY SUPPLEMENTED THEIR MEAGRE
WAGE WITH WEEKEND JOBS AT A
TAILOR'S SHOP FREQUENTED BY
LOCAL ARMY OFFICERS.

moulins

IT WAS AS A SEAMSTRESS THAT
GABRIELLE CAME INTO CONTACT
WITH MOULINS MILITARY MEN
WHO WERE LARGELY DRAWN FROM
FRANCE'S LANDED GENTRY AND
PARISIAN ARISTOCRACY.

DELIGHTING THE OFFICERS WITH
THEIR VIVACIOUS PERSONALITIES,
GABRIELLE AND ADRIENNE WERE OFTEN
ESCORTED TO CAFE-CONCERTS.

THESE SHOWS WERE PART OF
A GROWING TREND FOR BAWDY
ENTERTAINMENT, WHICH STARTED
LIFE IN BELLE EPOQUE PARIS.

GABRIELLE WAS DRAWN TO THE
STAGE AND BECAME A POSEUSE —
A GIRL WHO WOULD FILL THE GAPS
BETWEEN BILLED ACTS.

SHE WOULD SING REVUE STANDARDS
'KO KO RI KO' AND 'QUI QU'A VU
COCO?' THE NAME 'COCO' STUCK.

Qui qu'a vu Coco

vous n'auriez pas vu Coco? Coco dans l'Trocadéro

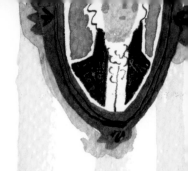

COCO BECAME INVOLVED WITH ONE OF THE CAVALRY MEN. ETIENNE BALSAN WAS A WEALTHY BACHELOR WITH A TALENT FOR BREEDING AND TRAINING HORSES.

HIS DISTINGUISHED FAMILY DESPAIRED OF HIS LIBERTINE LIFESTYLE AND OPEN DISREGARD FOR SOCIAL CONVENTION.

IN SEARCH OF FAME AND FORTUNE, COCO LEFT MOULINS FOR NEARBY SPA TOWN VICHY. DESPITE SINGING LESSONS, INVESTING IN FANCY FROCKS AND TRYING TO IMPRESS NUMEROUS STAGE MANAGERS, HER DETERMINATION CAME TO NOTHING.

COCO WAS ALONE AND WITHOUT
AN INCOME. IN 1905, SHE TRAVELLED
NORTH TO OISE TO BECOME ETIENNE'S
LIVE-IN MISTRESS AT HIS NEW HOME,
CHATEAU DE ROYALLIEU.

'I was nothing but a lost child.'

ROYALLIEU WAS A PLAYGROUND.
FRIENDS AND THEIR MISTRESSES
WOULD COME FOR THE PARTIES,
HUNTING AND HORSE RACES.

ETIENNE TAUGHT COCO TO BE A
SKILLED HORSEWOMAN AND, WITH
BOHEMIAN FLOURISH, SHE HAD A PAIR
OF JODHPURS MADE FOR HERSELF.

IT WAS THE AGE OF THE COURTESAN
AND COCO SHARED THE CHATEAU
(AND ETIENNE) WITH ONE OF THE
ERA'S MOST EMINENT GRANDE
COCOTTES, EMILIENNE D'ALENCON.

Emilienne

UNLIKE THE LAVISHLY BEJEWELLED COURTESANS AND FEMININE MISTRESSES, BOYISH COCO HAD NEITHER CURVES NOR A FONDNESS FOR OSTENTATIOUS SILKS AND FURS.

SHE WOULD TRIM HER OWN STRAW BOATERS AND WEAR MODEST, TAILORED OUTFITS.

DESPITE ETIENNE'S FRIENDSHIP AND
PROTECTION, COCO GREW RESTLESS.

'I would say to myself over
and over, money is the key
to freedom.'

AFTER THREE YEARS TOGETHER,
ETIENNE GIFTED COCO USE OF
HIS PARIS APARTMENT AT 160
BOULEVARD MALESHERBES.

USING IT AS AN ATELIER, COCO
MADE HER UNCOMMONLY SIMPLE
HATS AND SUCCESSFULLY SOLD THEM
TO THE COCOTTES AND ACTRESSES
SHE HAD MET AT ROYALLIEU.

DELFT BLUE BEADS

WHITE
GEORGETTE
CRÊPE

BRAIDED WOOL

BLACK SATIN

BLUE AND
BLACK RIBBON

CERISE YARN BRAID

CERISE RIBBON

PHEASANT FEATHERS

STRAW HAT

BLACK VELVET

A SKEIN OF SILK

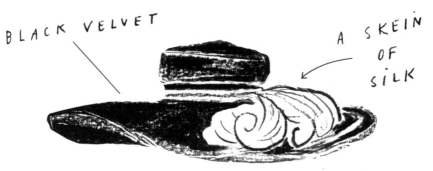

ARTHUR 'BOY' CAPEL LIVED NEARBY. THE YOUNG, RICH ENGLISH PLAYBOY AND 'LION OF LONDON SOCIETY' HAD MET COCO THROUGH ETIENNE.

THE PAIR'S SUBSEQUENT AFFAIR LEFT HER ENTANGLED (BOTH EMOTIONALLY AND FINANCIALLY) WITH TWO MEN. BOY PREVAILED, AND IN 1909 COCO MOVED INTO HIS PARIS APARTMENT.

AS COCO ESTABLISHED HERSELF,
HER TWO SISTERS TOILED. TO HELP
ANTOINETTE, COCO INVITED HER TO
WORK AT HER ATELIER. BUT SADLY
JULIA-BERTHE COMMITTED SUICIDE
IN 1910, LEAVING BEHIND HER
ORPHANED SON, ANDRE PALASSE.

GABRIELLE ASSUMED RESPONSIBILITY
FOR HER NEPHEW, LOOKING AFTER HIM
IN PARIS BEFORE ENROLLING HIM IN BOY'S
FORMER BOARDING SCHOOL IN ENGLAND.

SHE WOULD REMAIN CLOSE TO ANDRE,
SPENDING SUMMERS WITH HIS FAMILY
WHEN HE WAS GROWN UP.

FIN-DE-SIECLE PARIS HAD BECOME A
BEACON OF MODERNITY, WITH ITS GRANDE
BOULEVARDS AND MIGHTY ARCHITECTURE.
FASHIONABLE SOCIETY WAS IMPRESSED
BY THE LATEST TRENDS.

FINANCED BY BOY, COCO OPENED
HER FIRST STORE AT 21 RUE CAMBON.
ACTRESSES BEGAN SPORTING HER
CUTTING-EDGE HATS IN MAGAZINES
AND STYLISH SOCIETY WOMEN
QUICKLY FOLLOWED.

COCO'S RELATIONSHIP WITH BOY
(AND HER TRADESWOMAN POSITION)
ENSURED SHE WAS OUTWARDLY
SHUNNED BY THE ELITE PARISIAN
CIRCLES HE MOVED IN. BUT HER NOVEL
LIFESTYLE MADE HER STRIPPED-BACK
HATS ALL THE MORE TALKED-ABOUT.

COCO ALWAYS STOOD APART.

SHE WAS KNOWN FOR THRUSTING
HER HANDS UNCONVENTIONALLY
INTO HER POCKETS.

DESPITE BOY'S INFIDELITY, HE AND COCO WERE IN LOVE. HE ADMIRED HER TALENT AND DETERMINATION, AND ENCOURAGED HER IN BUSINESS, HELPING HER OPEN SHOPS IN THE SEASIDE RESORTS OF DEAUVILLE (1913) AND BIARRITZ (1915).

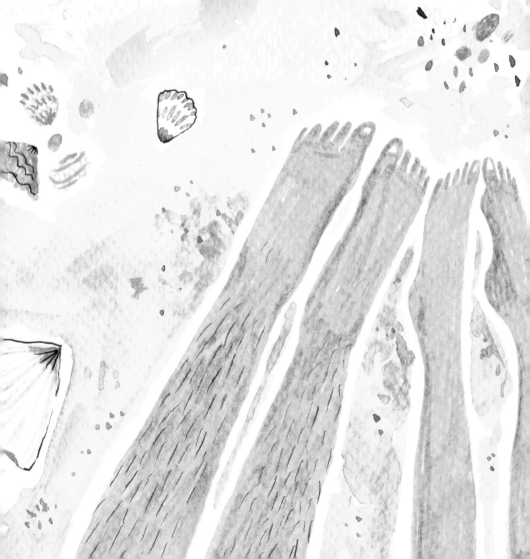

IN REACTION TO THE FLAMBOYANT, CORSETED STYLES AND DECADENT MATERIALS OF THE ERA, COCO STARTED INTRODUCING EASY-TO-WEAR SEPARATES WITH SPORTY, MASCULINE AND UTILITARIAN INFLUENCES.

'Over-embellishment had stifled the body's architecture.'

HER COLLECTIONS WERE PERFECTLY TIMED FOR A COUNTRY PLUNGED INTO WORLD WAR ONE IN 1914. THEY WERE PRACTICAL, FLATTERING AND FITTINGLY AUSTERE (THOUGH IN REALITY THEY WERE BOTH EXPENSIVE AND EXCLUSIVE).

'To look once at a Chanel jersey costume
is to desire it ardently.'

Vogue, 1916

HER MINIMALIST COLLECTIONS
WERE MADE OF CHEAP JERSEY.
THIS INNOVATIVE, ANTI-LUXE
APPROACH GAVE HAUTE COUTURE
A WELCOME JOLT.

BUSINESS BOOMED AND COCO
FOUND THE FINANCIAL INDEPENDENCE
SHE HAD LONGED FOR.

IN 1917, COCO DARINGLY
CROPPED HER LONG HAIR.

BOY SIGNED UP FOR ACTIVE SERVICE, THOUGH OFTEN VISITED COCO WHILE ON LEAVE. HE ALSO FOUND TIME FOR AN AFFAIR WITH ENGLISH ARISTOCRAT DIANA WYNDHAM.

BY THE END OF THE WAR IN NOVEMBER 1918, BOY'S ROMANTIC WRANGLE BETWEEN THE TWO VERY DIFFERENT WOMEN WAS OVER. HE'D CHOSEN TO MARRY DIANA.

1918 ALSO SAW 35-YEAR-OLD COCO EXPAND HER PARIS BOUTIQUE TO A LARGE SALON AT 31 RUE CAMBON. BUT BOY'S ABANDONMENT LEFT HER BROKENHEARTED.

COCO ESCAPED PARIS TO A RENTED
VILLA IN THE CITY'S SUBURBS. DESPITE
HIS NEW MARRIAGE, BOY STRUGGLED
TO GIVE HER UP. BY SPRING 1919
HE WAS BACK IN COCO'S ARMS.

THEIR RENEWED ROMANCE WAS
CUT SHORT ON 22nd DECEMBER
1919 WHEN BOY'S CAR OVERTURNED
BEFORE EXPLODING INTO FLAMES.
HE WAS 38.

ON THE DAY OF THE FUNERAL, COCO INSTEAD VISITED THE SITE OF THE ACCIDENT. SHE WALKED AROUND THE BURNT CAR WRECKAGE AND SAT WEEPING ON THE SIDE OF THE ROAD.

'in losing Capel, i lost everything.'

COCO WAS EMOTIONALLY SHATTERED. HER CLOSE FRIEND MISIA WAS SOON TO MARRY SPANISH PAINTER JOSE MARIA SERT. COCO JOINED THE NEWLYWEDS ON A RESTORATIVE TRIP TO ITALY.

SHE VISITED MUSEUMS AND
CHURCHES, JUNKSHOPS AND SALONS.
SHE FELL IN LOVE WITH THE ART
AND ARCHITECTURE.

MISIA MOVED IN BOHEMIAN CIRCLES AND SOON COCO BECAME FRIENDS WITH THE ERA'S MOST AVANT-GARDE ARTISTS INCLUDING PABLO PICASSO.

Picasso

COCO WENT ON TO FUND SERGEI
DIAGHILEV'S REVIVAL OF 'THE RITE
OF SPRING' BY THE RADICAL BALLETS
RUSSES IN 1920.

SHE ALSO DESIGNED COSTUMES FOR JEAN COCTEAU'S PLAY 'ANTIGONE' (1922) AND THE BALLET 'LE TRAIN BLEU' (1924).

Le Train Bleu

COCO LOVED CLEANLINESS,
CAMELLIAS AND LIONS (HER
ASTROLOGICAL SIGN WAS LEO).

SHE BELIEVED THE NUMBER 5
BROUGHT HER GOOD LUCK.

HAVING JOINED FORCES WITH EXPERIMENTAL PERFUMER ERNEST BEAUX, COCO LAUNCHED HER FIRST FRAGRANCE IN 1921. THE PIONEERINGLY COMPLEX SCENT (IN A UNIQUELY MASCULINE BOTTLE) WENT ON TO MAKE HER MILLIONS.

BETWEEN 1921 AND 1924, COCO
HAD SEVERAL AFFAIRS, SOMETIMES
OVERLAPPING. FIRST, THERE
WAS MARRIED COMPOSER IGOR
STRAVINSKY, FOLLOWED BY EXILED
RUSSIAN DUKE DMITRI PAVLOVICH.

SHE HAD A BRIEF LIAISON
WITH PICASSO, AND A DEEP AND
TURBULENT AFFAIR WITH HIS FRIEND,
THE POET PIERRE REVERDY.

'My love life got very disorganised,
because the person i loved had died.'

THE JAZZ AGE WAS BEGINNING
TO SWING, AND CAFE SOCIETY
FAVOURED RAUCOUS BAR LE BOEUF.
IT WAS COCO'S REGULAR HAUNT,
FILLED WITH THE FASHIONABLE
AND FABULOUS.

WHILE OUTLANDISH DESIGNERS
PAUL POIRET AND ELSA SCHIAPARELLI
HAD A BIG IMPACT ON THE ERA'S
FASHION, COCO LEFT A MORE LASTING
LEGACY. HER EASY ELEGANCE ALLOWED
A WOMAN'S PERSONALITY TO TAKE
CENTRE STAGE: A PHILOSOPHY
EMPHATICALLY DEMONSTRATED BY HER
MOMENTOUS LITTLE BLACK DRESS.

'Eccentricity was dying out;
I hope, what's more, that I
helped kill it off.'

IN 1924, COCO EMBARKED ON AN AFFAIR WITH THE DUKE OF WESTMINSTER (NICKNAMED BENDOR) — ONE OF THE RICHEST MEN IN ENGLAND.

THEY SPENT THEIR TIME HUNTING ON HIS SCOTTISH ESTATE, CRUISING ON HIS YACHT AND ENJOYING THE GLAMOUR OF THE FRENCH RIVIERA.

A DEMON WITH A FISHING ROD,
COCO WOULD REEL IN SALMON
AND TROUT ALONGSIDE BENDOR
AND HIS CLOSE FRIEND,
THE FUTURE PRIME MINISTER
WINSTON CHURCHILL.

COCO'S TIME WITH BENDOR
INSPIRED HER WORK. HER 'ENGLISH
LOOK' DREW HEAVILY ON THE BEAUTY
AND PRACTICALITY OF HUNTING
JACKETS AND YACHTING ATTIRE,
FEATURING BESPOKE SCOTTISH TWEED,
NAVY SHADES AND GOLD BUTTONS.
IN 1927, SHE OPENED A SHOP IN
MAYFAIR, LONDON.

The English Look

NOW IN HER LATE 40s, COCO FAILED
IN HER ATTEMPTS TO GET PREGNANT
AND BENDOR WOULDN'T CURB HIS
INFIDELITY. BY 1930, THEIR AFFAIR
HAD COME TO AN END.

AS THE GREAT ECONOMIC
DEPRESSION TOOK HOLD, COCO SET SAIL
FOR HOLLYWOOD WHERE FILM PRODUCER
SAMUEL GOLDWYN AGREED TO PAY HER
$1 MILLION A YEAR TO DRESS HIS STARS.

camellias

Coco's

a string of pearls

shearing scissors

lipstick

Boy's portrait

perfume

N°5 CHANEL PARIS

threads

Atelier

Lion sculpture

pins

bracelets

buttons

notes

cigarettes

MORE AFFAIRS FOLLOWED, INCLUDING
A DEEP ONE WITH ILLUSTRATOR PAUL
IRIBARNEGARAY, A BRIEF ROMANCE
WITH SALVADOR DALI AND RUMOURED
LESBIAN LIAISONS.

COCO HAD AN ENVIABLE SOCIAL LIFE
AND ENJOYED HER PUBLIC ADMIRATION
(PARTICULARLY FROM THOSE WHO ONCE
THOUGHT HER LOWLY). BUT ALONE AT
NIGHT, SHE WOULD INJECT A MORPHINE
SEDATIVE TO HELP HER SLEEP.

ON 3rd SEPTEMBER 1939, FRANCE
DECLARED WAR ON GERMANY. A FEW
WEEKS LATER, COCO CLOSED THE
HOUSE OF CHANEL (LEAVING ONLY
31 RUE CAMBON OPEN). NINE
MONTHS LATER, THE NAZIS
ADVANCED INTO PARIS.

THE OCCUPATION CHANGED
EVERYTHING AND THE GERMAN
COMMAND BECAME PART OF LIFE.
THOSE WHO DIDN'T GO INTO EXILE
OFTEN FOUND THEMSELVES OBLIGED
TO WORK FOR THE OPPRESSORS.

DURING THE WAR, COCO ENTERED
INTO AN AFFAIR WITH HANS GUNTHER,
BARON VON DINCKLAGE. SHE ALSO
EMBARKED ON A FAILED ATTEMPT
TO SET UP PEACE TALKS BETWEEN
CHURCHILL AND THE GERMANS.

THE AMBIGUITY SURROUNDING
HER ACTIONS LEFT HER REPUTATION
IRREVERSIBLY TARNISHED.

Von Dincklage

WHEN THE WAR ENDED IN THE SUMMER OF 1945, COCO MANAGED TO AVOID THE FATE OF MANY 'HORIZONTAL COLLABORATORS'. THESE WOMEN WERE PARADED NAKED THROUGH THE STREETS AND HAD THEIR HAIR SHAVED OFF.

JUST MONTHS LATER, COCO RETREATED TO SWITZERLAND. SHE KEPT A LOW PROFILE FOR NEARLY TEN YEARS.

WHILE SHE WAS AWAY, FASHION IN PARIS WAS FAMOUSLY TRANSFORMED.

Dior's

New Look

COCO FELT THAT ALL HER HARD WORK
HAD BEEN UNDONE BY CONTEMPORARY
DESIGNERS LIKE CHRISTIAN DIOR AND
PIERRE BALMAIN. THEY SEEMED TO LOOK
TO THE PAST FOR THEIR INSPIRATION,
AND THAT CAUSED COCO TO OPENLY
RAIL AGAINST THEM.

THE RESTRICTIVE, HOURGLASS
SHAPES AND RETURN TO THE ROMANTIC
IMAGE OF FEMININITY WAS CONTRARY
TO EVERYTHING COCO HAD FOUGHT FOR.
WOMEN WERE AGAIN TRUSSED UP
IN COSTUME.

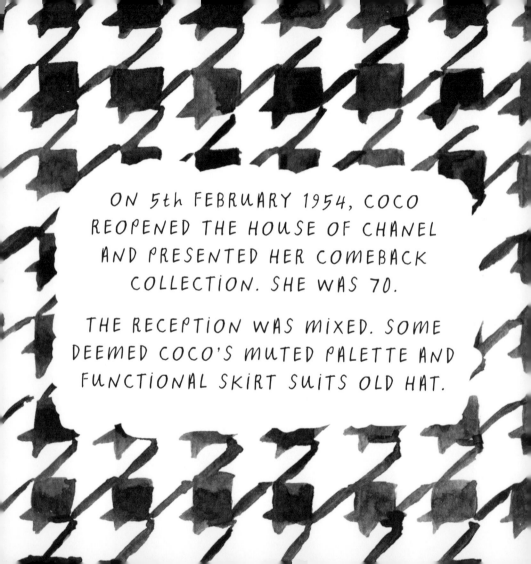

ON 5th FEBRUARY 1954, COCO
REOPENED THE HOUSE OF CHANEL
AND PRESENTED HER COMEBACK
COLLECTION. SHE WAS 70.

THE RECEPTION WAS MIXED. SOME
DEEMED COCO'S MUTED PALETTE AND
FUNCTIONAL SKIRT SUITS OLD HAT.

BUT AMERICAN VOGUE,
BRITISH BUYERS AND WOMEN THE
WORLD OVER UNDERSTOOD THE
COLLECTION'S TIMELESS APPEAL AND
THE IMPORTANCE OF THESE DESIGNS
IN A REFINED WARDROBE.

'I lived a modern life, I shared
the habits, the tastes and the needs
of those whom I dressed.'

OVER THE NEXT TWO DECADES, COCO
CONTINUED TO INNOVATE AND HER
POPULARITY WITH STYLISH, PRACTICAL
WOMEN NEVER WANED. HER DEFINING
STAPLES AND SIGNATURE, MUCH-
COPIED CREATIONS (FROM BAGS WITH
SHOULDER STRAPS TO COSTUME
JEWELLERY) HELPED HER ESTABLISH
A LASTING LEGACY OF ELEGANCE
AND EASY GLAMOUR.

earrings

WIDE
TROUSERS

STRAW

BOATER

2.55 *handbag*

pockets!

pyjama top

costume
jewellery

camellia
corsage

TWEED
JACKET

BRETON TOP

skirt
suit

Little
Black
Dress

pearl
necklace

AS THE YEARS PASSED, COCO BECAME
FRAIL. IN HER 80s SHE WAS PLAGUED
BY ARTHRITIS AND RHEUMATISM. BUT
DESPITE HAVING ALIENATED MOST
OF HER FRIENDS, SHE CONTINUED
TO FIND REFUGE, SOLACE AND
DISTRACTION IN HER WORK.

ON 10th JANUARY 1971, COCO COMPLAINED OF FEELING SUFFOCATED AS SHE LAY ON HER BED. HER MAID HELPED HER INJECT HER LAST PHIAL OF MORPHINE. SHE WAS 87.

'Anyway, that is the person I am. Have you understood? Very well, I am also the opposite of all that.'

Acknowledgements

Coco Chanel's history is difficult to pin down. Accounts of her life vary wildly, not least because she herself was apt to tell different versions of her own story. The author has taken care to be accurate and faithful to the truth throughout. There are, however, two scenes within the book which are known to be reported, rather than confirmed. First is the idea that the nickname 'Coco' was the result of Chanel singing revue standards. The second is the oft-reported account of her travelling to the site of Boy Capel's car accident on the day of his funeral.

For a wealth of biographical detail, the author would like to gratefully acknowledge the vivid and comprehensive *Chanel: An Intimate Life* by Lisa Chaney, as well as *Coco Chanel: The Legend and the Life* by Justine Picardie.

The illustrator would like to extend her love and thanks to Ali, Ma, Pops, Jojo and Chester.

All the quotations used in this publication have been sourced from the following title, with the kind permission of both Pushkin Press and Hermann:

The Allure of Chanel, Paul Morand (Pushkin Press/© 1976, Hermann).

This is with the exception of the *Vogue* quote, which was reprinted with permission from Condé Nast Publications.